This notebook belongs to:

_____

Published by: Character Designs

PROJECT/TEAM: _____   DATE: _____

PERSONA: _____   USER STORY/SCENARIO: _____

_____
_____
_____

_____
_____
_____

_____
_____
_____

_____
_____
_____

_____
_____
_____

_____
_____
_____

_____
_____
_____

_____
_____
_____

_____
_____
_____

RESEARCH NOTES:

_____

_____

PROJECT/TEAM: DATE:

PERSONA: USER STORY/SCENARIO:

RESEARCH NOTES:

PROJECT/TEAM: DATE:

PERSONA: USER STORY/SCENARIO:

RESEARCH NOTES:

PROJECT/TEAM: DATE:

PERSONA: USER STORY/SCENARIO:

RESEARCH NOTES:

PROJECT/TEAM: DATE:

PERSONA: USER STORY/SCENARIO:

RESEARCH NOTES:

PROJECT/TEAM: DATE:

PERSONA: USER STORY/SCENARIO:

RESEARCH NOTES:

PROJECT/TEAM: DATE:

PERSONA: USER STORY/SCENARIO:

_____   _____   _____
_____   _____   _____
_____   _____   _____

_____   _____   _____
_____   _____   _____
_____   _____   _____

_____   _____   _____
_____   _____   _____
_____   _____   _____

RESEARCH NOTES:

_____
_____

PROJECT/TEAM: DATE:

PERSONA: USER STORY/SCENARIO:

RESEARCH NOTES:

PROJECT/TEAM: DATE:

PERSONA: USER STORY/SCENARIO:

RESEARCH NOTES:

PROJECT/TEAM:

DATE:

PERSONA:

USER STORY/SCENARIO:

RESEARCH NOTES:

PROJECT/TEAM: DATE:

PERSONA: USER STORY/SCENARIO:

RESEARCH NOTES:

PROJECT/TEAM:

DATE:

PERSONA:

USER STORY/SCENARIO:

RESEARCH NOTES:

PROJECT/TEAM:

DATE:

PERSONA:

USER STORY/SCENARIO:

RESEARCH NOTES:

PROJECT/TEAM: DATE:

PERSONA: USER STORY/SCENARIO:

RESEARCH NOTES:

PROJECT/TEAM: DATE:

PERSONA: USER STORY/SCENARIO:

RESEARCH NOTES:

PROJECT/TEAM:

DATE:

PERSONA:

USER STORY/SCENARIO:

RESEARCH NOTES:

PROJECT/TEAM: DATE:

PERSONA: USER STORY/SCENARIO:

RESEARCH NOTES:

PROJECT/TEAM: DATE:

PERSONA: USER STORY/SCENARIO:

RESEARCH NOTES:

PROJECT/TEAM: DATE:

PERSONA: USER STORY/SCENARIO:

RESEARCH NOTES:

PROJECT/TEAM:

DATE:

PERSONA:

USER STORY/SCENARIO:

RESEARCH NOTES:

PROJECT/TEAM: DATE:

PERSONA: USER STORY/SCENARIO:

PROJECT/TEAM: DATE:

PERSONA: USER STORY/SCENARIO:

RESEARCH NOTES:

PROJECT/TEAM: DATE:

PERSONA: USER STORY/SCENARIO:

RESEARCH NOTES:

PROJECT/TEAM: DATE:

PERSONA: USER STORY/SCENARIO:

RESEARCH NOTES:

PROJECT/TEAM:

DATE:

PERSONA:

USER STORY/SCENARIO:

RESEARCH NOTES:

PROJECT/TEAM:

DATE:

PERSONA:

USER STORY/SCENARIO:

RESEARCH NOTES:

PROJECT/TEAM: DATE:

PERSONA: USER STORY/SCENARIO:

RESEARCH NOTES:

PROJECT/TEAM:

DATE:

PERSONA:

USER STORY/SCENARIO:

RESEARCH NOTES:

PROJECT/TEAM: DATE:

PERSONA: USER STORY/SCENARIO:

RESEARCH NOTES:

PROJECT/TEAM:

DATE:

PERSONA:

USER STORY/SCENARIO:

RESEARCH NOTES:

PROJECT/TEAM: DATE:

PERSONA: USER STORY/SCENARIO:

RESEARCH NOTES:

PROJECT/TEAM: DATE:

PERSONA: USER STORY/SCENARIO:

RESEARCH NOTES:

PROJECT/TEAM: DATE:

PERSONA: USER STORY/SCENARIO:

RESEARCH NOTES:

PROJECT/TEAM: DATE:

PERSONA: USER STORY/SCENARIO:

RESEARCH NOTES:

PROJECT/TEAM: DATE:

PERSONA: USER STORY/SCENARIO:

RESEARCH NOTES:

PROJECT/TEAM: DATE:

PERSONA: USER STORY/SCENARIO:

RESEARCH NOTES:

PROJECT/TEAM: DATE:

PERSONA: USER STORY/SCENARIO:

RESEARCH NOTES:

PROJECT/TEAM: DATE:

PERSONA: USER STORY/SCENARIO:

RESEARCH NOTES:

PROJECT/TEAM: DATE:

PERSONA: USER STORY/SCENARIO:

RESEARCH NOTES:

PROJECT/TEAM:

DATE:

PERSONA:

USER STORY/SCENARIO:

RESEARCH NOTES:

PROJECT/TEAM: DATE:

PERSONA: USER STORY/SCENARIO:

RESEARCH NOTES:

PROJECT/TEAM:

DATE:

PERSONA:

USER STORY/SCENARIO:

RESEARCH NOTES:

PROJECT/TEAM: DATE:

PERSONA: USER STORY/SCENARIO:

RESEARCH NOTES:

PROJECT/TEAM: DATE:

PERSONA: USER STORY/SCENARIO:

RESEARCH NOTES:

PROJECT/TEAM: DATE:

PERSONA: USER STORY/SCENARIO:

RESEARCH NOTES:

PROJECT/TEAM:

DATE:

PERSONA:

USER STORY/SCENARIO:

RESEARCH NOTES:

PROJECT/TEAM: DATE:

PERSONA: USER STORY/SCENARIO:

RESEARCH NOTES:

PROJECT/TEAM:

DATE:

PERSONA:

USER STORY/SCENARIO:

RESEARCH NOTES:

PROJECT/TEAM:

DATE:

PERSONA:

USER STORY/SCENARIO:

RESEARCH NOTES:

PROJECT/TEAM: DATE:

PERSONA: USER STORY/SCENARIO:

RESEARCH NOTES:

PROJECT/TEAM: DATE:

PERSONA: USER STORY/SCENARIO:

RESEARCH NOTES:

PROJECT/TEAM: DATE:

PERSONA: USER STORY/SCENARIO:

RESEARCH NOTES:

PROJECT/TEAM: DATE:

PERSONA: USER STORY/SCENARIO:

_____

RESEARCH NOTES:

PROJECT/TEAM: DATE:

PERSONA: USER STORY/SCENARIO:

RESEARCH NOTES:

PROJECT/TEAM: DATE:

PERSONA: USER STORY/SCENARIO:

RESEARCH NOTES:

PROJECT/TEAM: DATE:

PERSONA: USER STORY/SCENARIO:

RESEARCH NOTES:

PERSONA:

RESEARCH NOTES:

PROJECT/TEAM:

DATE:

PERSONA:

USER STORY/SCENARIO:

RESEARCH NOTES:

PROJECT/TEAM:

DATE:

PERSONA:

USER STORY/SCENARIO:

RESEARCH NOTES:

PROJECT/TEAM: DATE:

PERSONA: USER STORY/SCENARIO:

RESEARCH NOTES:

PROJECT/TEAM: DATE:

PERSONA: USER STORY/SCENARIO:

RESEARCH NOTES:

PROJECT/TEAM: DATE:

PERSONA: USER STORY/SCENARIO:

RESEARCH NOTES:

PROJECT/TEAM: DATE:

PERSONA: USER STORY/SCENARIO:

RESEARCH NOTES:

PROJECT/TEAM: DATE:

PERSONA: USER STORY/SCENARIO:

RESEARCH NOTES:

PROJECT/TEAM: DATE:

PERSONA: USER STORY/SCENARIO:

RESEARCH NOTES:

PROJECT/TEAM: DATE:

PERSONA: USER STORY/SCENARIO:

RESEARCH NOTES:

RESEARCH NOTES:

PROJECT/TEAM:

DATE:

PERSONA:

USER STORY/SCENARIO:

RESEARCH NOTES:

PROJECT/TEAM: DATE:

PERSONA: USER STORY/SCENARIO:

RESEARCH NOTES:

PROJECT/TEAM: DATE:

PERSONA: USER STORY/SCENARIO:

RESEARCH NOTES:

PROJECT/TEAM: DATE:

PERSONA: USER STORY/SCENARIO:

RESEARCH NOTES:

PROJECT/TEAM:

DATE:

PERSONA:

USER STORY/SCENARIO:

RESEARCH NOTES:

PROJECT/TEAM: DATE:

PERSONA: USER STORY/SCENARIO:

RESEARCH NOTES:

PROJECT/TEAM: DATE:

PERSONA: USER STORY/SCENARIO:

RESEARCH NOTES:

PROJECT/TEAM: DATE:

PERSONA: USER STORY/SCENARIO:

RESEARCH NOTES:

PROJECT/TEAM: DATE:

PERSONA: USER STORY/SCENARIO:

RESEARCH NOTES:

PROJECT/TEAM: DATE:

PERSONA: USER STORY/SCENARIO:

RESEARCH NOTES:

PROJECT/TEAM:

DATE:

PERSONA:

USER STORY/SCENARIO:

RESEARCH NOTES:

PROJECT/TEAM: DATE:

PERSONA: USER STORY/SCENARIO:

PROJECT/TEAM:

DATE:

PERSONA:

USER STORY/SCENARIO:

RESEARCH NOTES:

PROJECT/TEAM: DATE:

PERSONA: USER STORY/SCENARIO:

RESEARCH NOTES:

PROJECT/TEAM:

DATE:

PERSONA:

USER STORY/SCENARIO:

RESEARCH NOTES:

PROJECT/TEAM: DATE:

PERSONA: USER STORY/SCENARIO:

RESEARCH NOTES:

PROJECT/TEAM: DATE:

PERSONA: USER STORY/SCENARIO:

RESEARCH NOTES:

PROJECT/TEAM: DATE:

PERSONA: USER STORY/SCENARIO:

RESEARCH NOTES:

PROJECT/TEAM: DATE:

PERSONA: USER STORY/SCENARIO:

RESEARCH NOTES:

PROJECT/TEAM: DATE:

PERSONA: USER STORY/SCENARIO:

RESEARCH NOTES:

PROJECT/TEAM:

DATE:

PERSONA:

USER STORY/SCENARIO:

RESEARCH NOTES:

PROJECT/TEAM:

DATE:

PERSONA:

USER STORY/SCENARIO:

RESEARCH NOTES:

PROJECT/TEAM:

DATE:

PERSONA:

USER STORY/SCENARIO:

RESEARCH NOTES:

PROJECT/TEAM: DATE:

PERSONA: USER STORY/SCENARIO:

RESEARCH NOTES:

PROJECT/TEAM:

DATE:

PERSONA:

USER STORY/SCENARIO:

RESEARCH NOTES:

PROJECT/TEAM: DATE:

PERSONA: USER STORY/SCENARIO:

RESEARCH NOTES:

PROJECT/TEAM: DATE:

PERSONA: USER STORY/SCENARIO:

RESEARCH NOTES:

PROJECT/TEAM: DATE:

PERSONA: USER STORY/SCENARIO:

RESEARCH NOTES:

PROJECT/TEAM:

DATE:

PERSONA:

USER STORY/SCENARIO:

RESEARCH NOTES:

PROJECT/TEAM:

DATE:

PERSONA:

USER STORY/SCENARIO:

RESEARCH NOTES:

PROJECT/TEAM:

DATE:

PERSONA:

USER STORY/SCENARIO:

RESEARCH NOTES:

PROJECT/TEAM: DATE:

PERSONA: USER STORY/SCENARIO:

RESEARCH NOTES:

PROJECT/TEAM:

DATE:

PERSONA:

USER STORY/SCENARIO:

RESEARCH NOTES:

PROJECT/TEAM:

DATE:

PERSONA:

USER STORY/SCENARIO:

RESEARCH NOTES:

PROJECT/TEAM:

DATE:

PERSONA:

USER STORY/SCENARIO:

RESEARCH NOTES:

PROJECT/TEAM: DATE:

PERSONA: USER STORY/SCENARIO:

RESEARCH NOTES:

PROJECT/TEAM: DATE:

PERSONA: USER STORY/SCENARIO:

RESEARCH NOTES:

PROJECT/TEAM: DATE:

PERSONA: USER STORY/SCENARIO:

RESEARCH NOTES:

PROJECT/TEAM: DATE:

PERSONA: USER STORY/SCENARIO:

RESEARCH NOTES:

RESEARCH NOTES:

PROJECT/TEAM:

DATE:

PERSONA:

USER STORY/SCENARIO:

RESEARCH NOTES:

PROJECT/TEAM: DATE:

PERSONA: USER STORY/SCENARIO:

RESEARCH NOTES:

PROJECT/TEAM:

DATE:

PERSONA:

USER STORY/SCENARIO:

RESEARCH NOTES:

PROJECT/TEAM:

PERSONA:

DATE:

USER STORY/SCENARIO:

RESEARCH NOTES:

PROJECT/TEAM:

DATE:

PERSONA:

USER STORY/SCENARIO:

RESEARCH NOTES:

PROJECT/TEAM: DATE:

PERSONA: USER STORY/SCENARIO:

RESEARCH NOTES:

PROJECT/TEAM: DATE:

PERSONA: USER STORY/SCENARIO:

RESEARCH NOTES:

PROJECT/TEAM: DATE:

PERSONA: USER STORY/SCENARIO:

RESEARCH NOTES:

PROJECT/TEAM:

DATE:

PERSONA:

USER STORY/SCENARIO:

RESEARCH NOTES:

PROJECT/TEAM: DATE:

PERSONA: USER STORY/SCENARIO:

RESEARCH NOTES:

PROJECT/TEAM: DATE:

PERSONA: USER STORY/SCENARIO:

RESEARCH NOTES:

PROJECT/TEAM: DATE:

PERSONA: USER STORY/SCENARIO:

_____

RESEARCH NOTES:

PROJECT/TEAM:

DATE:

PERSONA:

USER STORY/SCENARIO:

RESEARCH NOTES:

Takeaway notes:

_____

_____

_____

_____

_____

Year of use:

_____